"Shirlette Ammons proves over and over again that 'poetry is a think-ing woman's job'. She snatches an array of cultural, historical, and contemporary materials to conjure the assurance of her dangerous genius." JAKI SHELTON GREEN

"Shirlette Ammons writes with fierce abandon, but not without con-trol. Her poetry will put your tongue through its paces, unjumble the junk in your brain, and point out your internal organs (this is your heart; this here is your gut). These poems honor all kinds of truths: the loud and the quiet ones, rich old truths, and newly unleashed truths. She speaks your language, but makes it all her own. From Goldsboro, North Carolina to Flatbush, Brooklyn and beyond, black women appear in all our complexity: as 'amateur amazons...wet with winced whisky,' as the much-admired 'militant' cousin who 'got a afro and a lesbian for a girlfriend,' as a 'Rocking chair raconteur / ... Seeming southern / and seeking things.' I can't say enough about the joy, incisive wit, unpretentious honesty, and illuminating imagery in this book—but I can say too much, because here you are still reading my words when you could (should!) be reading Shirlette's!" EVIE SHOCKLEY

MATCHING SKIN

Shirlette Ammons

CAROLINA WREN PRESS
Durham, North Carolina

Editors: Tanya Olson and Andrea Selch
Design: Lesley Landis Designs

The mission of Carolina Wren Press is to seek out, nurture and promote literary work by new and underrepresented writers, including women and writers of color.

Earlier versions of the following poems appeared in Shirlette Ammons' *Stumphole Aunthology of Bakwoods Blood* (Big Drum Press, 2002): "Ain't No Shame in Matching Skin," "Sub-Goldsboro Garage Gals," "Militant Black Women," "History Makes Concessions for White Boys," "Fender Bender," "Mother Beaneater," "Revisiting Baraka's Preface," "Slick Shit," and "Playing Woman."

"Census Man Cometh," was first published in *The Ringing Ear: Black Poets Lean South* (University of Georgia Press, 2007)

This publication was made possible in part by generous grants from the North Carolina Arts Council and the Mary Duke Biddle Foundation. In addition, we gratefully acknowledge the ongoing support made possible through gifts to the Durham Arts Council's United Arts Fund.

Library of Congress Cataloging-in-Publication Data
Ammons, Shirlette.
Matching skin / Shirlette Ammons.
    p. cm.
A collection of poetry, along with CD soundtrack.
ISBN 978-0-932112-56-9
1. African Americans--Poetry. I. Title.

PS3601.M65M37 2008
811'.6--dc22
2008012496

DEDICATION

To my pops, June Fitzgerald Hamilton.
"Juju said it ain't the seeds
Then he said it's in your roots
And I believed"

I ain't no high yella, I'm a deep killer brown.
I ain't gonna marry, ain't gonna settle down.
I'm gonna drink good moonshine and rub these browns down.

BESSIE SMITH,
YOUNG WOMAN BLUES

CONTENTS

THE WAY WE PLAY (FLUNG THIGH LEFT)

JOHN ANONYMOUS (ALSO ON CD)

AFTERWORD

THANK YOU

TRACK LISTING

PRIMER

The High Un-Lonesome of Shirlette

High lonesome is a sound. A piercing, high-pitched, solo harmony, made famous by guitar-picking, banjo-playing, story-singing, men and women of the Appalachian region of the country; Dolly Parton, Bill Monroe, Ralph Stanley, both Docs, Boggs and Watson, and Loretta Lynn are some of the best known. The high lonesome is a sorrow song that sizzles out of the tops of long leaf and yellow pine; a sound that celebrates hard times, good-bad love, and the razor-sharp edge between the old ways of living and the new. From North and South Carolina, through Kentucky, into West Virginia and beyond, the notes of high lonesome have pierced the airwaves of this country for many a generation, but mainly from across the tracks, on the white folks' side of town.

In some strange but powerful way I'm connected to the high lonesome. I have been since I was a girl. I didn't know other black girls drawn to this kind of sound, when I first heard it, so throughout my life, mostly, I have kept quiet about my peculiar affinity for it, even though I know it has made its way into my work like molasses on the back of the tongue. Over the years, I've written and talked about why a Southern black girl might be so deeply moved by this kind of twanging guttural octave, but *Matching Skin* by Shirlette Ammons is the train crossing where both sides of the track come together.

Shirlette Ammons is a poet with a piercing, high-pitched, solo-harmony sound. But it is not the high lonesome that she sings. Her poetry is not sad, depressed, maudlin, reclusive, sequestered, estranged, forsaken, forlorn, or, I-am-without-a-friend-in-the-world. Shirlette's sound is that of the high un-lonely, the securely, emotionally-trenched and tethered. She is the pure sound of the well-anchored bare feet, the pounding, inquiring, well-moored, southern+black+female, inquisitive heart. She is the young black woman sipping hand-cut peach juice with five fingers and picking a fiddle with the other five. She has the high worldly knowledge of an independent woman, one who knows the secrets of how to grow food in the sun and the shade. She has that blouse-unbuttoned-at-the-top, poetic, sensual presence; a woman unafraid of what the human body can and should feel and share with another human body, while also brandishing the traditional white-napkin-in-her-lap good manners. This soulful, gravy and biscuit goodness, this barbeque smoky sweetness, inherent to Southern life and necessary to the poetry of that landscape, is central to Ammons' lyrical voice in this, her second book.

Turn the pages here and you immediately hear the pluck of hard-strumming African banjoes, leaping out from 1845. You hear the smooth slide of African feet, walking, dancing, and sometimes running for their lives, without shoe the first. You hear harmonica solos and the irregular meter of holiness praise houses. Ammons is moving in this old red dirt on every page and leaving finger and foot prints, taking the back roads, because the view from there is ripe with natural old-time wonder and she is never alone, never. She has brought her people with her: Sarah Vaughn, Jimmy B, Amiri Baraka, Grace Paley, Nina Simone, Curtis Mayfield, Lightnin' Hopkins, Adrienne

Rich, Salt N Pepa, Dave Chapelle, Abbey Lincoln, and Gwendolyn Brooks. All legendary company and good traveling mentors for a young poet intent on rolling hard on the back roads until the road ends or something new begins or the hurricane hits.

The words on the pages are all hers, but the train she jumped off and the boat she climbed out, before she started singing solo harmony, were full of storytellers, moonshiners, and people who made long-lasting things with their hands. It's so obvious that good people, God-people, have raised her. These midnight-oil burning folks, do-the-right-thing, down-to-earth folks, have thrown their quilted padded arms about her so she might know lonely—might even write about it here and there—but never live lonely. They had to make sure she would never be found across the tracks, outside, under the full moon, wailing, trying to wear sorrow and tragedy like a black girl body sash. *No sir, not our Shirlette.*

Shirlette is not the high lonesome—and neither am I. Perhaps we are poets who require the presence and the down beat of the high lonesome, in order to understand what we is and what we ain't, in order to craft and create our own high un-lonely sound in the world. Ammons is unique in the annals of contemporary poetry but she also comes out of a fierce tradition; the deep waters of speaking one's mind, following one's heart, and honoring the music of the words that make up that eclectic world called human response. Never the imitator, always originating new words for old feelings, she pulls grace and high notes from old watering holes and bait fields. Her new ways of saying are soon drying in the soft summer sun on her mama's clothesline. I listen in close because it's my mama's clothesline too, even though it's one entire southern birth-state and one entire black-woman generation away. When Ammons writes her succulent image-driven lines, she is naked as a jaybird, splashing hard in every puddle wanting to feel the power of every liquid drop. It is hard to mistake her for what she is: a well-read poet unafraid to use the word *militant* in 2008, in order to describe nothing and everything about herself. Ammons is cardinal and radical in her posh and purposeful alignment of words: "she fireant pissed and her skirt simply won't sit down." In her fearlessness of fact on the page, she stomps and curtsies and does not wait for any applause: "A black girl playing woman/Is destined to be somebody's momma." She is sweeping in her side looks and exquisite in her full sensuous address of taboo temporal love: "a spread of crescent moon/ shine/ a touch of promises kept / up her sundress." She is loving and instinctive in her read and embrace of family. Her looking around at the world is rich, with an even richer, freethinking mind, and passion-rich heart. Her immodest, immoderate stories sit me up straight in the sweetgrass woven night chair, there to transition me from nighttime to dream state. Her words are the strong hands at my back. Her language gifts me a new set of eyes for old old heartbreak. By dawn the book is closed and I am grateful for every alphabet.

Shirlette Ammons is a black Southern girl singing the high unlonesome blues in 2008. On the page her songs need breath and ear, un-tied and clicking tongue rage and engage, in order to hope out loud that the reader will come in close, fill every corner of their mouth with her warm butter and soft loaf of words, then take a heart full of satisfaction, provenance, fullness, and feeling on up the road. Everything she tells is told with her hands on her hips and her arms akimbo—*Aunt Lou is blooming like a radiant lobelia. The census man cannot keep up with the spelling of the family's name. Uncle Johnny and Uncle Buddy are dead and black folks ain't shame of noth-*

ing. If we pay attention, her words strike the match of what she is afraid of but does not fear. She is aural, oral, and augur. Her words glisten with crickets, squawking roosters, jaybirds, and become a hot summer zephyr whipping through a field of tobacco leaves. She knows the power of nicotine but keeps it, mostly, under her tongue. She will ride you where you don't really want to go. There are canoes, j boats, and quiet rafts, waiting at the edge of her streams of metaphor. This young musician-poet is a card-holding torch singer for sunflowers, slop jars, jazz, swine, and family lore. She's not a preacher but she could preach if she had to. If living in a truer world depended on it. She would pull out a cardboard collar and sport it with no problem. *Don't make me go there,* her line breaks whisper. *There, that's enough of that,* her titles bat their eyes once, then leave you and the poem in the small bright room alone to think about what's been revealed, that should have been talked about long ago. She knows the church. She's been on the front and back row tapping her foot. She's been inside the Book of John—wandering *anonymously.* The cadence of deep spirit is clear in her line-humming titles and chapter breaks, but she will not be chained to any pew. She will not be affixed to what you think she should know or be—or say. Sometimes there is need for every poet, worth their salt, to float high up to the eaves and rafters in order to see the world more clearly and speak more fearlessly. No problem there.

"there's a lot of us"

In her first collection, *Stumphole: Aunthology of Bakwoods Blood,* and now again in *Matching Skin,* Shirlette Ammons, poet, exhibits her abstract expressionistic style. Her love of balladry, the human voice, and narrative is unmistakable. Her black country music leaves the ear and heart aching and ringing out, mad, and smelling like sour apple wine spilled in Uncle Junior's new, black leather, back seat. The same jaw that has been punched has also been kissed and held. The deep holding of one's own self, strong and tight, is ongoing, until the arms of a trusting other finally arrive. Her positioning of family, local, personal, and world history is the beautiful stained glass through which her words stream. This reservoir of living is where the un-lonesome first fermented. This wise, young, hungry poet, writes what she must write, and never hesitates to ask, request, beg, the hundreds of hearts and souls that have fed her throughout her life, to come and puppet her fingers up and down on the page, one more time. There are, indeed, *a lot of us* who need her words out in the whirlwind of this world. Include me in that number.

Nikky Finney
Northampton, Massachusetts
March 2008

AIN'T NO SHAME

*If you scheming on the chance to put a
stain on my name
Don't even think about it cuz ain't no
shame in my game.*

GANGSTAR,
AIN'T NO SHAME IN MY GAME

Ain't No Shame in Matching Skin

Po folk can't shame a balding ground
vermillion sunshine blinds black backs
shanty shacks shade ashy elbows
holding poses on haltered hips
southern eyes squint like breathing cracks
sharp minds too shy to invent
dingy young uns see no sadness in
shielding dark faces from matching skin

Po folk see rainbows in bald ground
pause from play like dreams made real
stripped and striped, deep ebony to light
wells churn their truths like whippoorwills
fellowship rings like gospel hymns
sisters, brothers, cousins count most
they all must be the chosen one
shielding dark faces from God's sun

Po folk talk to a balding ground
lard buckets leak like grease music
rhythm got feet, it walks around
pushing big toys with plastic wheels
a gritty earth records the sound
oh yes, we making music now

fusing backwoods with cricket's song
knew that shame wouldn't last too long

Po folk make love from balding ground
grow into your face, identical pose
hold me closer, sweet better half
don't wash away our dingy soul
claim your sunshine, brush your lips
cover your smile to lock love in
save your own dreams from turbulence
switch your hips for me, Matching Skin

Living Will

Uncle Buddy went before his hog's last feedin,
Uncle Johnny behind a discount cigarette;
Cut'in Citty Ruth withered just before
hookin her last bait
three jobs for twelve mouths
made Grandaddy's heart explode

Gramma, too tired to keep up, asked I
swathe her feet with camphor;
I prepped her bruised embers,
seen em crumble to soot as I massaged

Aunt Lou's the youngest of the old,
she comes home to fireworks on the Fourth,
pig pickins and prodigal patriot bouquets;
she is the lobelia Beautancus planted in Peoria
savin obituaries, savorin Budweisers
like flimsy bookmarks in *Our Daily Bread*

On the fifth, she packs her '70s Samsonite,
back to frying family recipes for Illinois Gamma girls;
no homefolk can see her now
hovering over that sorority house stove;

she shifts her weight to a walking cane,

toasts the last day her siblings wore work shoes

We are a family darned and patched;

like hearty hand-me-downs

from Mr. Julius to his son Lanny,

we made for sturdy work clothes

in the ceremonial South

the living bequeath the living

over secret handshakes at the coolin board

Roberta is Working Clergy

Roberta works the Savior's packing line
pearled in purple choir curtains and citrus sponge curlers
she and The Word perch on slaughtering surfaces
slaying Satan and singeing curt breathing from early cocks
Roberta is The Blood, The Way, The Water

In the break room,
Lance chips and honey buns wait with TD Jakes
Roberta binds the sweets in thin slices of Scripture,
gurgles, urgently, her nurturing need, *Lord,*
Have Mercy on your working Durga, she pleads;

Bosses, *Hell-bound Heathens,* she calls them,
mimic her calling, curse her unskilled altar
yet, they gather, the fishes and the loaves,
at the feet of her cock-slit pulpit
eager to be dismantled,
like the gizzard from the giblet,
The Word, their perfect minimum wage

Before break time unburdens its serpents,
lurking with demerits & demotions,
The Spirit splays like disobedient turkey gall

she stays, Rahab amidst the loosened walls of Jericho,

to gird the Unlearned hurrying to The Promised Land

Roberta benedicts the persecuted,

from God's forgone turf, they disperse

on the brink of the briny Jordan

the scarlet rope saves her page,

she approaches the throne of Herod

to receive her scalding

burning in faith for tomorrow's crossing

Sub-Goldsboro Garage Gals

a woman's body is the universal shelter
JUNE JORDAN

Propped in sleek recline,
chipped cinder loafs as amateur amazons
scan hooded vehicles for leaky lubricants,
a grimacing Gran Torino,
glued grounded by a gluttonous gasket,
greets a girlish sub-Goldsboro gang
who done graduated to grassy garage gals
since Granddaddy's gone

Buried beneath this weak wreckage,
women wet with winced whisky
wear wild weekends to weather workday weariness;
they rear a wedlocked litter
wrenching a rusty, worn oil filter
with a family of phallicless, faultless fingers

Round where wheat lice weeds and winds,
washpots wait on wood heaters to warm winter water
warning weary women who wear make-do wisdom
to wade every once in a while

Militant Black Women

My cousin is older than fifty;
she got a afro and a lesbian for a girlfriend,
she got sense, too;
she stayed up late-nights to school me
cause she figured I need her very particular feelings
about country crackas;
them folk wont ready to deal
with the size of her world,
Black and suspiciously bold
like the image I got of her and her afro
ridin down Ole Kenansville Road
roundin them curves with the nerve
to coast down the ripest black thighs;
and since my cousin got sense, she turned militant
and, omitting the details, I figure
radicalism had her admitting
Black chicks was *where it's at*
when you need to be understood, otherwise
you'd think your ownself crazy for tryin
to get educated beyond the backwoods;
now we sit, talking bout everything but details,
I listen, wondering if I have inherited
the conniption to stroll Ole Kenansville Road
scoutin tobacco fields for militant black women

History Makes Concessions for White Boys

From all my white sins forgiven, they feed
PHILLIP LEVINE

At the Food Lion,

this cute one hangs and guts

the pot-bellied pork;

I suppose his kisses salt and slime

which would have appeased the high school me;

ham gelatin swathing my tongue

as I lipsynced "Good Vibrations"

like Mark Wahlberg wasn't just

a white boy in dropped boxers

protesting the mullet

I remember his face now,

he and his girlfriend mashed like Juicy Fruit

in that big-ass, dixie-flagged, Ford F-150

me, a member of the yellow school bus gang,

sitting, suffocating, three-deep in a pleathered seat;

Mexican, Black, Po White Trash, cousins of cousins

muddled like the fuzz between pecan trees

and AM radio stations;

her hands, gold nugget promise rings,

engaged his stringy hair;

as his dual mufflers fumed down Highway 403,

racial divide scoured the windshields
of our wheeled, county property

He steps outside between slaughterings
to smoke a red-boxed Marlboro.
I notice his bangs have grown out;
he stares as if my locks carry remnants
of barrettes and blurred bus numbers;
we nod and smile, an understood country greeting;
I figure he and his girlfriend still coast cramped,
the same way public transportation taught us
to squeeze tight in our assigned seats
in case the white boy's pickup broke down

Why else would we make room for a passenger
who never needed a ride?

Fender Bender

I call them road trips
as if the tar stretching out
dark as Goshen Swamp
really cares to take me
to my sister safely;
when I get there,
I will wake her
to say goodnight
then retire to my breath
and whatever rests upon it;
I will ask myself
where I have been, and, if
for some reason,
I will need to be there again;
in either case,
I left a gaze in the rearview
like disturbing notions
of never getting old
and each time
I thought I was wiser
ignorance could ram me
like a deer, blindly but boldly,
(which I respect)
darting out in front of me

so I close my eyes and scream

God bless me

this to the same God

who, moments before

forged His identity

inside the radio

before I started spiraling

and blaspheming blessings;

but now my neck hurts

like there's a cramp lurking

and I got this bruise on my arm

that I rub unconsciously

and the soreness sits

like a blueprint in the fold

of my forearm and elbow

so when my knees meet the carpet

I will remember to give thanks

while wearing the pain.

Twister of '86

Like a screen door
made of inside and out
it pounded and opened
fell forward and in
backwards and beyond
and Dewayne could only see it
as a spinning exit
like when Daddy spit out the Jehovah's Witness
cause sometimes God ain't looking

The trailer rooftop, masticated guts
the whole family, chitlins on a flagellant fork
the belly of the beast bites with
no particular appetite
the trailer village digested:
mother's pale skin is a tossed salad
relentlessly tumbling
father is spiraling spaghetti
Dewayne's marinara hair is molten and crunchy
noodling through the twister's esophagus

Late for dinner,
their own natural disaster

Gramma Thunder

Date: Sun, 9 Feb 2003 11:50:30 -0800 (PST)

From: "shirlette ammons" View Contact Details

Subject: Gramma Thunder

To: Nikky Finney

my gramma used to sit in her favorite chair, housecoat
wide open...open down to in between her leftover
breasts...she ain't weigh no more than a mosquito
lookin for blood, but her body was bold and lean...i
seen her tote a foottub-load-a ashes out the heater
with the grace and balance of a broom sweep...how her
breasts kept pulling down but not showing up...the
divots dug up, turf torn and sucked, babies swelling
in her sweet, sweaty nipsap...the tawny, cleavageless
gap nuzzling thirteen needy knaps...the baby girls
tugging swifter than the boys, her tits like ready
weaponry, loaded, poised...

> *give me all i got / coming to myself / so that when i finally*
> *if ever stop / you really know / that this time / she has truly*
> *come and gone*   NIKKY FINNEY

Food Stamps

Ma'am,
I am standing directly on the yellow line.
the line looks backwards and ahead;
cars drive through me because I am thinking
right here in the middle of Need Mo Street
listening to myself being crushed underfoot;
I will move,
I will scrape myself from the pavement
(when I am less busy)
I will walk to Gramma's in summertime
and curl my hair in hot comb heat
I will chew bacca and dip snuff
cause I always wanted caramel spit;
I will dance in my bag of secrets
cause poetry is a thinking woman's job,
like welfare is poetry
and waiting in WIC lines is, too;
Ma'am,
poetry don't ask for a thinking woman's income
so why the hell do you?

Census Man Cometh

for the Ammons family tree

Census Man cometh
countin mulattos muddlin round
dirty wit Duplin County's scarlet gravel
redbone Americans, able-bodied
but under the table
pedalin good comp'ny and cathouse calls

Way downeast,
arrowheads and horseshoes welcome
like placemats on porch fronts
beneath the front door stuck under a doorstep
on a bent nail is a doorbell—
betta not step on it if you don't want
none-a Boogieman's bad side

Shack smoke stacks soot on census records
unrecorded whores wit delicious dancin hips
press against piano, no pianist
he stumpdrunk and humpin the cat
dead on the pantry flo
next to Unc's left four-fingered hand,

which, when bent by the kerosene lamp,

licks the last sip of city gin

from the five-string guit' strummin sweet while

Aunt Eleeza's main squeeze's bed keeps squeakin

she fireant-pissed and her skirt simply won't sit down

Unc wake up lookin for his 5th finger

and Census Man knees keep creakin and crickin cause

he simply won't sit next to a thumb that can't be found

dime liqua and them Ammons women

make Census Man forgit his numbas every time

and this what he scribbled on his way up County line—

In 1784, '86, and '89,

Them Ammonses spelt they names

Difurnt ways at difurnt times

There was Everit in Piney Grove

Who threw a —d there on the end

And Zachariah in '90

Went and took it off agin

Now I ain't got no problems

Wit fellaship and citygin

But, seem like them Ammonses

Is messin up my scribbulin
But they's sho is some purty colors
Shimmerin beneaf they skin
Look like next Sat'day nite
I'll be back countin em agin!

I FANCY SARAH
WHO NEVER
CLAIMED JAZZ

Sending mournful soulful sounds
soaring over trouble grounds

ABBEY LINCOLN,
BIRD ALONE

I Fancy Sarah Who Never Claimed Jazz

Niggas is quick to turn they backs on spittas wit clits
JEAN GRAE

Spinderella's not a fella / Spinderella's dope
SALT N PEPA

The waiting, when flicked,

dawns like a first cigarette

emcees tilt lids and cup dicks

dragging Levis by the knees

Less than a foyer's worth of us,

girls with our own steel chins,

hadn't fucked the locally famous;

our patience and tits

wilting like early perennials

in sullied sports bras

A taut band of tough breeds

eyes certain like slicing surgeons,

resume whet with Latifah's wrath,

weighed the stakes before

filing the application

I fancy a remix of Sarah's scats

over broken Spinderella beats

a requiem for dare dames

improvising orgasmic rants

setting off a stage stampede

And When You Become Abbey

on Abbey Sings Abbey, *by Abbey Lincoln*

And when you become
a stylist of Triptych scream
the black moan in jim crow's craw
when you take the Anne out
your name and blame the
absent system, not the song
when your lyric swings low
out-belting the everyday firing range
when the double barrel and
driva'man be damned
you, fortified by your own catalogue,
brassier the second time you sing yourself
when you benedict in blue notes
and your birthstone is a work song,
triple daring and straight-ahead,
when your broad brim leaps
like seventy-seven sleek leopards
and your brooch lines a golden throat
pinned to your own breasts headed
South and Southside

when your spine rises out of a meow

growling a gritty scat

and your hand holds a fifty-two card deck of

spades and mangled face cards

and your wrinkles holster a discourse

for drumsticks

when your grandkids are jazz bastards

and you hug them with your whole mouth

and collect scratched vinyl for them to play

like piano keys

Mother Beaneater

For Gwendolyn Brooks

All I know about her
is glasses thick enough
to be spectacular
and a dictionary filled
with carmine and castaways
from Bronzeville

When I see
how broad her face
I know how tasteful
poetry pulsates
to wash clean
with swollen rags
heavy eyes
with sleepless bags

I can learn across
her pear-shaped ether
like honeysuckle knows
to grow in season
til vacant like tin cans
of the mostly beaneaters
How fair her exclamation

intense like a dream
of peeling ceilings
when her glasses sit clinging
to a desk organized
with messy meaning

I hope to rupture one day
to criticize the cancers
that plague
and write the breath I breathe
on a prolific sleeve
til my lungs sit punctured
with conception

Silueta: Sonnet-Ballad for Ana Mendieta

Her plaintive plaits, like a snake's shape, spiral
birthed in dusk from brown leviathan song
Cuban cunt framed in figurine tower
Silueta spindling ash and black skulls

Eight millimeters, like a needle's thread,
sketch mud meshed with massacred silhouettes
tribal opus choking on ocean bed
white with fire, a weeper's pyre portrait

Acrylic diary, laments in mire,
body parts breaking like gunpowder vials
spat thirty-odd stories, the orphaned child
silhouette battered like camouflage eyes
her plaintive plaits, like a snake's shape, spiral

Revisiting Baraka's *Preface*

> *And each night I count the stars*
> *And each night I get the same number*
> AMIRI BARAKA

Lately I've become accustomed to the way

Friday's spoken word employs an orgy of metaphors,

some a ménage of monogamous mind fucks,

others, broke-pencil-point prostitutes;

forced and forged freestyles

bored of their own torturous oration,

lords of encores no one asked for

as if ten dollars at the door deems

lyrical rambles nonperishable

Things have come to that

The sky blinds me as I nightwalk through the dark

knowing the stars take part in my seeing,

except the stage is the limelight tonight

so, even I, coveting the number

of poems twinkling in dusty anthologies

am not looking up, am not counting

The holes they leave

And then last night I tiptoed up

inside the boiling brown of a literary caldron

white with Wheatley's malnourished lips,

speaking easy an ashy English

stewing a vocabulary of double standards

before renaissance requests we write them down;

found myself feeling not-so-contemporary,

knocking the tedious junk

that innovates and materializes our lives

at an unforgivable high speed

The ground opens up and envelops me

as I leave behind the hollow *snap snaps*

of another spoken expression

knowing no one was listening except my

Own clasped hands

Storyteller

How did this happen / Well that's who I wanted to be
GRACE PALEY

Rocking chair raconteur
pitching to a creaking porch's tenor
rants on about things non-urbane
eyes like palps, ears like spiracles,
senses wiry and gaping
like a grasshopper's anatomy
hot-winded from abdomen to thorax

A milieu of plastic and masking tape
wrinkles over a window she once fixed
as a tattling child of grace and gravel
field-flaunting and almost free

She sways
and the world in her radius
is fables and fingertips
returning to dust;
she drawls away the space
between pasture and passing
to mend a remedy home

Like a cloud
light as a curl of hair,
her punchy stature
stews the horizon
in an instant
she moves beyond
seeming Southern
and seeking things

Do the Funny

For Dave Chappelle

Stand up
Sit down
Hold on
Hurry up
Make the funny do

Here come the hose
The flog will
Masturbate the funny
Right outta you
Do the Bubba Blue
And the hose wont whip you
Do the Bubba Blue
And we'll give you
55 million funnys

For 55 million funnys
He'll do the Bubba Blue
Don't matter how Muslim his black
He will pixie for 55 million funnys
The funny aint cheap
Whatchu think

We gone give you

55 million funnys

For free?

You aint but

One funny

Can be traded

For another funny

Who'll do the Bubba Blue

Your funny aint all that

And a bag-a Sammy Davis

Yo funny is just

Rick James, bitch

For frat boys

Every black funny know

Norbit don't get

55 million funnys

For social satire!

Yes.

Nutty Professor got

55 million funnys

For Bubba Blue

And Shrek donkey

Didn't you learn this
In black funny school?

Did you just say
You wont do the Bubba Blue
For 55 million funnys?
Did you just say
55 million funnys
Cost too much?

You must be smokin
Funny cigarettes

For Harry Whitaker:
Whole Other Me of Jazz

I called the album Black Renaissance *because that it what
I wanted to see happen—especially in music. I've told some
people about it over the years. Now they can actually hear it.
It was a record before its time.*   HARRY WHITAKER

I had this whole other me of jazz

out there on a ledge. Headless torso

being water with the rest of the psychedelics,

toting a shitload of twisted tongues

late notes brung to me in a bad shape,

late notes seeking composite arrangement

and my ubiquitous black ass was fast to oblige

every djembe, every symbol, every bassline

tainted with the pre-weight of Donny's 300-pound

depression. Damn that dude carried

a overloaded soul. Went straight out the window,

mad wit melody's sweet sardonic serenade. He

surrendered and left Flack crazy ass seekin

a musical dick to ride, some fool to eulogize

her cruel overindulgence. Man, fuck that! Where

I'm at is out there on the edge of the jazz in me, sittin

at the end of the jam waitin for the girls to scream

like they seen a alien in negro drag—draggin a new

beginning, apocalyptic. Yeah, that chick was brilliantly

insane. Tryin to claim the ground I been holdin for

forty years since. But, back then I was too headstrong to make

myself clear. They gone be groovin to my myth for ages,

way after the wailin river arranges me a date with that

faithful trumpet sound. Shit, ask Miles. I was rappin then

the same way I'm rappin now. And even he know my

weaknesses ain't never got me stuck in some musical

flux where I ain't have no business bein. Man, fuck that! Where

I'm at is out there on the edge, headless orchestrating hero

of the jazz in me.

Slick Shit (poetry practice)

onomatopoeia: slick words
euphony: sweet words
allusion: words wit tendencies
visual imagery: eye candy
auditory imagery: ear candy
gustatory imagery: rain-licked dirt
verbal irony: the way it is vs. the way it should be
repetition: repetition

slick shit don't stick to lint in black light

like words / these words that shimmy and shine

shaping my short term into loose-leaf cause

this be my homework /

verbal irony

shhhhhhhhhhh / roommate sleeps late

staples backside to pillows and nitemares

breathes stale oxygen like crunchy onion rings

this late / this early

neither can be legal

sloppy shopping thru thesauruses makes me

turn up the radiation

vj's push stale MTV dialect

must be the time taking the jive out

my people's mouth

flashes of miles in spain shellac / slapping me
into jazz dripping epiphanies
i know why them jazz cats found the dragon
the music burned in they bones /
they was on fire

yep
it's late cause I'm licking lint from my
spit-shined sheets / ain't been next to nuthin
in weeks / shameful miles. your horn says
you are lonely

ever had to pee so bad
then the piss hit the pan
that's poetry at its peak
I aint got no pen
(repeat)

similes ain't for poets cause
poets see things as they is
not as they like
emcees make rhymy words
resemble similes / deceive the masses

when it's early like sunrise and coffee
my teeth stain themselves / remember
tasting razor-sharp words wit
busy tongues

words are slick / they eat out my stool
shit out my food / love me til morning
then leave me alone.

THE WIND
HAS RISEN

On the stormy sea
Jesus speaks to me
and the billows
cease to roll

MANIE P. FERGUSON,
BLESSED QUIETNESS

The Wind Has Risen

...the wind will rise / we can only close the shutters
ADRIENNE RICH

The procession begins

as abrasive brass

cutting the body loose

a big easy dirge belted by

a grave, brackish breeze

the somber swells of,

Oh beh beh like gulf water

gurgle beneath second line sarongs

everybodys Aunt Trina

forwards the parade

carnival krewes and camera

crews and cumulus clouds spiked

with holy trinity cruise Esplanade

supercells sing raspy like Satchmo

the treble lends its tremor

to the bass in the brass

brattling against an iris playing bashful

each note, hot hips haltering

the hymn in the throat,

the tape-draped window

must be a shutter, a wreath of

fleurs-de-lis falling in a voyeur's forest,

on ears untreated, undisturbed

the dance, a march whirring, a

ripped roof trampling through

Tremé, rousing, a paradise depressed,

desperate celebrity yields a lewd forget

an aerial view on mute

God and damned flying from

the same stained glass

The wind has risen,

the shutters have fled the building

Boycott

The plant / The field chant / The fearfully underpaid parent / The
projected fire / The threat / The closing in and up / The influx of
stuck sixteens on diplomaless corners / The Sean John jean / The
overprice / The high stake / The stick used to loop / The cotton
gin / The absolute vodka

/ The sin / The forgiveness / The murdering man / The holy waging
war / The southern jumpable border / The censored patriot / The pre-
emptive act / The hands dealt / The dealer / The drug / The medicine
for the hands we've become

/The wrongs / Our rights / The leftover bruises / The health insur-
ance / The unaffordable cure / The stupid son (so the standards
say) / The discriminating hold-him-back factor / The factory wit no
window / The fishin for sunlight / The minnows thrown back if there
were time to relax / The packs of six and cigarettes instead

/The disease, the black lungs / The chain smoking gun / The aging
smock / The deferred dream / The stuck rut / The shut in my face
front door / The unemployment office / The late payment / The lights
out / The notice of eviction / The hopeless lump in the throat / In the
breast, cancerous spread of helplessness

/ The festering amen / The witness to the crime / Against the wall, my back / The gross pay / The grocery list ripped in half / The rift between lovers / The problem in the mouth without a name / The take home / The FICA / The food stamp / The waiting / The WIC line / The nigga / The spick / The cracka's tobacco / The agri biz / The big biz / The buyout / The sell out / The deficit / The embezzled sweat / The plaintiff / The defense / The decision / The sentence, cheap labor

/The skin game / The sifting through / The soil / The field manned by calloused hands / The spoils to the rich / The toils, the poor / The fear of finding out tomorrow don't exist / The exit sign / The beginning/The end of

Dying in and closing up / Stuck
Sucked in like hungry young stomachs
And varicose veins from standing still
Still standing
Standing
Still.

An Undulating Home

*After seeing a photo of a dead man perched in a lawn chair
outside the Convention Center in New Orleans. He looked
paused and let alone.*

Small the waves

shrinking like me

I am shrinking

in this room

where the walls

have pushed me

to the center

of myself

Take my hands

and wrap them

around my voice

in my pocket

is my cut throat

torn from my feet

tucked in my stomach

left to dry

dismantled for the dark

I live on display

while an early moon

struggles to pick me up
panic in its forced hand

I don't care to luggage
my self unzipped
let me wade or lay
with the trampled
folded away
like botched travel plans
on a map of no place to go

You Got the Dozens

This deviant dozen / won't go wholesale / born as puzzled parts of
speech / dukes tapped / witty sting / tongue bladed/like a fresh edge
up / this world / jokes and jeers / jaws agape / some black body /
gotta avenge the eaten asses / keep scrambled the semantic / sway of
us

That's why yo daddy get lost for a livin / handcuffed and operatin
with one headlight / darky in night traffic / That's why yo momma
so sad in the mornins / her face look like a damp washrag / that's
why you got so many families / all mashed up like hands in potata
salad / so much whatchu got / that snicker / sewed like a holy quilt /
all patchy and braided / warming the blue bone / coating the teeth
with blabber / you need that fuel / you bound to get snapped on /
real misfits slant hardluck like slang to stop them tears swellin / tell
em bout they own momma / snap pitches above that rebel yell /
poke them with your rolling eyes/plug yo ears and sing Simone's *aint
got no* / so when they snap/aint nuthin missin/you aint never had

Snap
Watch the trick door
Give way

The Ghost That Weaves and Bobs

for Raleigh First Fridays

Nice evening to ride
past R&B sweatshops stocked stiff
blunt heat humped beneath Hargett hoodies
past First Friday shit-talkers
swishing freestyles like hiphuggers
hip hop's cream crop holds late-nite, invite-only
stalled RPD mount and raggedly ride Harrington's mortar
billy-club security keeps "the peace" pistol-whipped,
like a Sunday-evening drag queen,
the on-the-clock trot is nervous,
cops watch cock-eyed,
mounted on hi-horses, costumes starched
sweat drippin the reins,
sizzling infernos drool drunken cover tunes,
Cardinal taxis track forth and back, taxed
the tarmac flatlines—last call
lushes lugged like human luggage
sluggishly clutch tender clits and crotches
palming three nimble minutes of nothing at all
Hargett Street hangs low tonight,
tar reaming off one-ways,
wasting sad eyes on bar maidens

catering to the way-muted music lounges

What a real nice evening to ride

the ghost that weaves and bobs loves old-school,

staggers home moaning, groping a lonely FM dial

How to Castrate Swine

These the boys we don't keep
for breeding
too small-minded,
won't practice restraint
too clabbered,
like the butcherous odor
bridled beneath the birthright
of a brash young boar

These the ones will become
cocksure cowards
made sturdy from
slouching sow tits,
strapping jerks in jockstraps,
stocky on steroids
and stolen foremilk;
treating such tainted meat
reeks offensive,
sharpen the scalpel,
the first incision follows
the tensing of the scrotum's skin

They will writhe like face-off
at the start of the contest

howling in the huddle

their own mothers' name

the testes will be heaved

from their colossal, growing tale

they will sober—guaranteed;

leave the crimson vessel uncut,

the hallucinations will instantly cease

The first testicle, tugged and twisted,

begging to exhume lost dignity

as the second is seized the same

Resolutions

Every new day
tends to the past
that is its cargo
that is its charge
successes are luggage
shortcomings are lugged
and we traverse with bags
of both

What is Grass?

All of it—
the tin roof on Trinity Avenue
where the clouds sit and scheme
a seventy-degree Durham
before the heat peaks

A neither bad nor good morning

The Britneys, the Burmese,
a track champion halved and veined,
criminal attempts at concerned media
scribed by typewriters with filthy keys when

We all have medals we should return

The grass is a mattress for our trampling
whisking us past overdue fines and late fees,
oh shits and honest-to-god forgets
as we beg to get clipped
like a thief preying on sickly screen doors
in the beam of broad daylight

THE WAY WE PLAY (FLUNG THIGH LEFT)

Baby dontchu tear my clothes
baby dontchu tear my clothes
You can push me, pull me all night long
But, baby dontchu tear my clothes

LIGHTNIN' HOPKINS,
BABY DON'T YOU TEAR MY CLOTHES

Boy Clothes

Force-fitted into loose flannel
these breasts, a heavy appendage
Southern fledgling heads west
wearing nothing but
a knot in the throat and
a harmless dildo flung thigh left,
practices a fragile bravado
for the Frisco prowling place

A crisp pussy scent
trails boygirl bathroom stalls
dykes stinking of Stetson
fluff feathered shags
condoms junked in cocky pockets
useless as past apartment keys;
a Farrah Fawcett femme
in acid-washed Jordache
waiting to squeeze the soap
hands me the eye,
if I purchase her first Corona
I can practice future slow drags
but I promised Janet the first dance,
Jane Kennedy at least, when,

surrounded by hefty bag heat,
the Amtrak docked in New Orleans;
making love to black celebrity mirages
in a velvet layover motel

A place in need of pacific rinsing
beats just beneath my chest
fakes me out, heads down south,
throbs with the quake of God
as an ebony pole queen
slinks toward,
grinds into,
writhes beneath it;
an air-fuck sinful enough
to finger me clear cross California
slinking toward,
grinding into
writhing atop
her hallelujah call and response,

Drought-stricken as a Downeast mosquito
in a field of Carolina wheat,

drenched like work clothes

naked of my fag virginity;

The time it takes to come out

equals three thousand miles

Audible Darkness

Shaped and hidden
beneath her caramel curves,
within this cut-away flesh,
high with the stench
of my dripping palms,
my wrinkles look like
letters of the alphabet
misspelled and heavy
because the heart is a sloppy muscle
bleeding and weeping
as darkness cradles black girls
who don't fall asleep
til the lights are out
and the crescent moon is a candle
spitting wax on a cherry wood desk;

Two grown women,
perfumed and hazardous,
expire long before the flame wilts;
every *do not touch* sign
like the thick-lipped brush
of a skillful broom,
is swept against the dark
for night vision

til the burning ceases

and the preacher asks

Who wants to be saved

As I raise my hand

with boiling skin,

I do not feel the need

for salvation

Midnight Gal

She just a bite darker
than thigh meat
greasy gremlin-type ugly
deep in the night
when the sun
don't hit the mirror
her sullied underbelly
is perfect to sink beneath

She rids the earth of beauty
no chatter, no laughter,
sugarless handful of bitter teeth
through each leftover molar,
she releases hideous grunts
no malicious man's moan
can hide behind

Cresting her moon,
soon I forget
the slick film,
the sickening heat
my chest mashed atop
her muted scowl,

the one position
that won't wear me down

I swear, she a demon,
eyes wit nightmarish stares,
dehydrating semen
wit her crinkled, tight prune
I loose any respect
for lower parts of my self
my bulging package
(when desirous)
lacks discretion

The ceiling fan clicks,
lick, spit
her shitty taste
split before limp disdain
sunlights her midnight face

Closeted

We dipped into the corner
light hunched behind our coats
like condolences
from a scurry of winters we hurried
for the singe of this secret cuffed in
the hem; toward the kindling that heats up
cold; the unfixed ends slipped
in the pocket; for the pierce after
the pristine wind that came and went
like a nick across our delicate chins,
refreshing, but
we cannot pretend we were kids

We drank coffee in lieu of afternoon curfews,
time was pinched visits and refills sipped;
held still our work sentences
like petty criminals with no cause to
bleed or repent; extended tentative
index tips like riskless teens,
wincing at the needle could make us
kindred, but
we cannot pretend we were friends

I wasted a cringe on the drive home,
gave in once the coat hit the hanger
and the weather set in—clicked *send*;
the email symphony commenced
fine and quick like a spontaneous drizzle
rinsing off a chilly mist, less than a kiss,
a prick; less than a dent, a miss but
I cannot pretend I was innocent

Like wispy solicits only work for virgins
and fragile make-believes breed non-answers,
my rooms with walls and closets with creaks
house honest garments both comical and dirty

Since we are early girls, why waste our pretends

Playing Woman

Reduced from all capital letters,
I find myself in the midst
of living smaller than secluded,
tinier than four writing walls

I guess this is a good beginning

I watch the mirror
believing Baldwin,
a better woman than I
to confess that reflections
have been known to lie
but I consider myself
facing the truth
naked

If I could document
all the women I have played
would I know which to deem accountable
for this mural of mistakes?
if I forget to leave an apology
will she sincerely accept the blame?

If I find myself alone
like a wrinkling Zora,
coughing up everything
but the memory
will I embrace old age?

If I cannot absolve all the lovers
who showered me with uncertainty,
how will I keep my own taste buds
from souring?

A black girl playing woman
is destined to be somebody's momma
paranoid and waiting,
calculating every bruise,
accepting each desperate collect call,
beaming a scrapbook of basketball trophies
covering peeling panel
with white jesuses.

Bangles

Baubles bangles hear how they ring ching-a-lingle
CASSANDRA WILSON

She hands me silver bangles and says, Don't forget yourself.
SHIKHA MALAVIYA

That's her

A woman writhing in her own bronze jingle
with eyes independent and beating
like twin hearts

Jingling as if she swallowed Alabama wind chimes,
a chest of jimmied cuffs, a rough memory of
Marvin's *mercy me* and Marley's deepsweet dimples

Standing on the front porch torched by her own
lightening, thunder snaking her wrist,
a splash of vanity journeys her hips; in the
watery wind she waves at uncles who favor
a drink, a strike; and in the 'lectricity of that jingle,
her jet-black kiss

Enchanted glance and chanting fist
in copper jingle twine, coiled around my insides
like a music tattoo dipped in Cassandra and carmine

Coming Off the Drums

like the ruby water rimming Abyssinia / she bows without breaking /

gyrating to kebero improvisations / she is coming to travel me /

to atlas me with a griot's tongue / and feed me like yams to Oshun

the waiting seethes like semolina steam

Long Distance

When we were living

apart

in parts of cartons

and wholes of handbags

I worshiped your gunning

it was Jet Blue

and mad with reservations

it had pages so full

I felt like a scribble

I was a dot

on your N.Y.C.

you couldn't even—

I bet all my money

on how you couldn't

define a spell

and now I'm strolling to

your breathy pace

I change my schedule

you pencil me in

yet bill collectors

call your house

lookin for you

and you say

I ain't here
I'm in Flatbush
walking wide and
fast
with this country gal
like easy rain
drizzlin through my borough
and we laugh
after the dial tone—
been shackin up
ever since
I walked you down

About Us #1

And her mouths part
to cool the humid kiss;
sticks like Dixie Crystal or Karo
same type sweet
a child can't get over,

With their eyes, lips shut,
the sheets fall like rain
absorbed, she swore,
a million fingers tapped her back,
after arching for hours, she tenders
sweating with tactless greed
lens eyeing the pit, still lit, she opens;
a simple almond revealed
she toys the ridges until
she is swimming back to the seed
of her own body's beginning

About Us # 2

She stirs and
sticks to my
spoon-fed spine
intense as
a five o'clock
wake up call
bare bodied with
rifle-bruised shoulders
and riff-ridged belly
she moans and flips
triggering, expectant

My fingertips are blue degrees
plummeting her hips
warm as a fireplace finally
I am pulsing blood
racing towards her summons
shaping her sound with heat,
Heavy from hauling
weapons into war—
at ease.
Body bare of armor
she soon learns
to seduce
civilians

The Way We Play is an Inspiring Promise

a spread of crescent moon shine /

a touch of promises kept / up her sundress /

a dance done to my sense

of taste / like Carolina pines smearing sticky

sweet sap / the texture of untied tongues

JOHN ANONYMOUS

There's a lot of us

Ain't it (A Shame)

What in the world is peace of mind
when pieces of minds define people's time
how in the world can we advance
when we can't define our own circumstance?
how in the world can we know love
when we got a closet full of skeletons
why in the world wait for change
when waitin for change don't change a damn thing
it's a damn shame, ain't it?

What does it matter that I got mine
if I'm leavin yours off on the sideline?
why does this world feel so alone
when everybody's got a cell phone?
and who in the world do we respect
if we can't recall in whose bed we slept
and why in the world strive for fame
strivin for fame don't change a damn thing
it's a damn shame, ain't it?

Juju Man

Juju man had his juju beans
I didn't know what they were for
says juju man to lil black ass me
what you doin next Sunday morning
I didn't have no plans
so me and juju man went
conjuring through the woods
and juju man was a left-handed man
so he knew right and wrong
was quite misunderstood
I wore my Sunday dress
he wore his Sunday best
his daddy (God rest his soul)
was part juju too
a wide-brim hat
with a feather pointed toward the past
was a hand-me-down
just like his three-piece suit
me nor juju man
was partial to the shade
cause we knew most shadows
were human made

so we laid in the grass

at the foot of a sassafras

sunlight as our compass

but we wont goin nowhere

Looking Glass

It ain't easy being needy
when you want nothing, have nothing
expect your best to be easily reflected
in your lifetime's looking glass
like something with eyes and it breathes
we stumble through reminders
we bottle, tuck, and tie
preserve love letters and calendars
marked with special events
fixed on holding on to life
like a looking glass

I turned on the news today
I heard a grieving mother say
can't nothing take her pain away
a woman down near Camp Lejeune
helped her husband pack his army suit
and in about nine months their baby's due

So can we take some time and listen
to what's in between the lines
before our state is our condition
can we make the time to try

Cause it ain't easy being needy

when you want nothing, have nothing

expect your best to be easily reflected

in your lifetime's looking glass

like something with eyes and it breathes

we stumble through reminders

we bottle, tuck, and tie

preserve love letters and calendars

marked with special events

fixed on holding on to life

like a looking glass

Tattooed Smile

Close to home as I been
you think I'd wanna go in
just to see how everybody's doin
but I'm starting to believe
won't nobody recognize me
cause my windows need cleaning
I can't even see through
if I sit here long enough
I won't even miss my youth
this smile is a tattoo
been wearing it for a long time
so when I ain't got nothing left
lay me down next to my last breath
tell the folks I loved I slept
on the steps but I ain't make it in

I'm just a child with a tattooed smile
too long forgot about
don't wanna go home
too long forgot about
and if somebody remembers me
ain't no guarantee
I'm-a be happy
cause happiness don't make you free

and I'm a child with a tattoo
cause my smile is a tattoo

I live at the end of a dead-end street
where all the dead ends meet
ain't got a lot to talk about
so I flip through the family page
remembering every age
scrambling to touch my family's face
but they only live in albums
sometimes it's hard to believe
folk don't see the pain on my sleeve
can't find relief in Momma's reprieve
cause Momma done and gone to Glory

So I sit in my dead end gloom
me and my tattoo
smiling to hide the blues
but ain't really nothing funny

I'm destined to be a man one day
as soon as I wipe this smile off my face
but what's so easy for you to see
ain't easy for me to say

so if you pray for me, I'll pray for you

that one day this tattoo

wont be the face I use

to keep me from my own reflection

John Anonymous

There ain't no once upon
that's just a literary fantasy phenomenon
something harmless
obedient to lines and corners

Like a battlefield with beautiful debris
fatalities no ceremony for the deceased
happily bury the masses
grind their bones to ashes
life flashes like bland snatches
of pictographs in fast-forward
no chronicle, no obstacles, or story
just onerous sound bytes
five parts poor plot
unoriginal word choices
suspense without climax
but you can't keep us from comin

What kind of jail cell
is a grayscale
where is my pandemonium
and my kaleidoscope
where is my rainbow coalition

association for colored folk

my overcome,

where is you at, huh?

I see the barbed wire

I see the statisticians

breakin me down into

lacerations and skewed percentages

I want my plot thickened

edit my paragraph

decipher every line

study me in English class

and then you do the math

I deserve a pretty name

something like crucifixion

or creative nonfiction

don't call me Section 8

my name ain't welfare

but I'll be a petunia

you can call me crystal stair

name me anomaly

you can call me chosen quilt

or just anonymous

there's just a lot of us

Afterword

The poems and music that precede coexist in this collection because they have inspired each other. While writing the poems in *Matching Skin*, I'd remember songs I had written years ago or begin shaping new ones. I would hum "Looking Glass" while writing "Roberta is Working Clergy" or "Living Will." Listening to the song "John Anonymous" inspired "Boy Clothes." This volleying between the poetry and music felt natural to me, even as I consider myself old-fashioned (Kai says I'm 'a purist') intrigued by the way art forms overlap and intertwine while reverent of the unique characteristics that make each expression its own. In a sense, *Matching Skin* is a composite of the *John Anonymous* EP and I am grateful to have them presented here together as kindred beings.

I also hope this collection of related poetry and music reveals my own personal tug-of-wars with identity, allowing my double-(triple-, quadruple-) consciousnesses to "meet and measure each other," as Emerson once wrote. I believe it is the evolution from double-consciousness to multiple-consciousnesses that instigates and helps resolve my own internal struggles and informs the art and actions of many of the artists of my generation—particularly the dissident ones. Therefore, these compositions are my small way of troubling our complacent yet multi-task-driven world.

Thank you

I would like to thank the following folks with whom I share in some form, a matching skin. I will think of a more suitable means of expressing gratitude, but, preserved here forever is a heartfelt appreciation. Visit it anytime you need to know your work, your ear, your art, your insight is invaluable.

Kai, you are an amazing woman and loving you is a commitment to laughter and slow dances. I admire who you are and love your appreciation of art as the story of our people. The way we play truly is an inspiring promise.

Momma, I love you for being like a new friend each day—interested in the woman I am becoming, inquisitive about my dreams and sharing yours.

Shorlette (Twin), I love our original matching skins. In our differences is where I am wowed by you—your love of gardens and books, your mothering of the most beautiful human I've ever witnessed (not you, Russell).

Anansi, I look up to you. Respect you so much. I hope you read these words and find in them a mystery for you to build upon as you grow and grow. I love being your aunt and an artist knowing that you are studying the world's every move—waiting actively on the horizon.

Shontae, thank you for being my family, my sister. Keep holding us up as you grow in your wisdom.

To my family: Momma, Jessie Mae, Lilly B, Annette, Rudy, Jean, Bobbie, Earlene, Aunt Lou, Tootsie, Tasha, Viv, Judy, Priscilla, Daddy,

Ush, Ross, Pedro, Buck, LJ, Ray, Billy, Jimmy, Roy, Russell, Keith, Nicky, Nae, Brandon, Josh (see Josh, you really can do anything). And all the new little offspring.

To the memory of Cousin Celia Ruth and Gramma Adell and every fishing bank where they sat a spell.

Andrea Selch and Tanya Olson, thanks so dearly for considering this work a worthy addition to Carolina Wren Press' catalogue. I am honored by your belief and support of me. Love to Evie Shockley, Lenard Moore and Jaki Shelton Green, and all those who've offered their words of encouragement. Chris Boerner, thanks for being my right hand. I believe in your compassionate approach to music. Thanks to Darion Alexander, Matt McCaughan, Caitlin Cary, Rhiannon Giddens, Greg Humphreys, John Teer, Adrian Duke, Daniel Hart, Hugh Swaso, and Brevan Hampden for offering your voices and musicality. You have breathed life into songs that have lain dormant in my spirit for almost too long.

Nikky Finney. I swear, I don't know what to say about the language you inspire and the tenderness of your ear, of your hand. I call, you answer like a cleansing breeze. Thank you for cradling me with your porch talk and your insistent belief in the word. I believe we match and that's reason enough for me to keep looking in the mirror.

A special thanks to all the nameless faces who have contributed to this collection in some way. I honor your voices, experiences and insights.

John Anonymous EP Track Listing

Produced by Chris Boerner
Mastered by Brent Lambert (The Kitchen, Carrboro, NC)

AIN'T IT
Music and lyrics by Shirlette Ammons
> Adrian Duke, vocals, Wurlitzer
> Chris Boerner, guitar
> Brevan Hampden, percussion

JUJU MAN
Music and lyrics by Shirlette Ammons
> Shirlette Ammons, vocals
> Greg Humphreys, background vocals
> Darion Alexander, bass
> Matt McCaughan, drums
> Chris Boerner, guitar

LOOKING GLASS
Music and lyrics by Shirlette Ammons
> Rhiannon Giddens, vocals
> Caitlin Cary, background vocals
> John Teer, mandolin
> Greg Humphreys, guitar

TATTOOED SMILE
Music by Shirlette Ammons and Greg Humphreys;
lyrics by Shirlette Ammons
> Shirlette Ammons, vocals
> Greg Humphreys, background vocals, guitar
> Daniel Hart, violin
> Brevan Hampden, percussion

JOHN ANONYMOUS
Music by Darion Alexander, Chris Boerner, Matt McCaughan,
Nic Slaton; lyrics by Shirlette Ammons
> Shirlette Ammons, vocals
> Hugh Swaso, vocals
> Chris Boerner, guitar
> Darion Alexander, bass
> Matt McCaughan, drums, Wurlitzer

The book was designed by Lesley Landis Designs